Unapologetically Raw: The Darkness Inside Her

AF624589

Miranda Holman

BookLeaf Publishing

Presentation by *BookLeaf Publishing*

Web: www.bookleafpub.com

E-mail: info@bookleafpub.com

ISBN: 9789357214780

First edition 2022

Thank you to all the strong women who have entrusted me to tell their stories with

dignity and pride. I applaud you for your courageousness, your encouragement, and your willingness to embrace the darkness and be unapologetically raw.

ACKNOWLEDGEMENT

Thank you to the editor of the following journal in which this poem, slightly differing in variation, have appeared or are forthcoming:

"Finding My Religion on A Deserted, Dusty Road in A White-Washed, Wooden Country Church" East Jasmine Review "Me Too" Anthology

PREFACE

“Someone I loved once gave me a box full of darkness. It took me years to understand that this too, was a gift.” - Mary Oliver

Tempest Queen

She was born of sunshine and thunderstorms
a combination of calm and chaos
she aches for the sparkle in the chaos,
yet yearns for the serenity before the storm.

Imposter

She planted a smile upon her thin, pale face, a masquerade she had been performing for too long. She laughed as her co-worker recalled a funny incident, although she wasn't listening to the meaningless chatter that consumed too much of her energy. She pulled her sadness back inside her empty body that once held passion and love and transformed into a performer putting on a show. She hid the invisible pain that screamed to be released as the unshed tears blurred her vision. Quickly brushing them away to mask the pain she counted down the hours until the veil of the imposter could be discarded.

Favorite Lip-gloss

I woke up today feeling a sadness surrounding
me,
a gut wrenching blow of loss and dissatisfaction.
A sadness that I know comes from the core
and not because I lost my favorite lip gloss.
A numbness flowed down my body
reminding me I sit empty and alone; Sterile?
My pillow became moist and I realized tears
were
Streaming down my face, yet I didn't feel
the wetness on my cheeks. Why today on this
sweet
Sunday morning with birds singing outside my
window? Bright rays of sunshine creating crystal
images on my hardwood floors. Why not
yesterday
when the sky was dark and the air was gloomy?
When you told me my love was no longer
needed.
You had found a new soul to love, a new body to
keep
warm on cold winter nights, like you kept me
warm
after our snowball fights. As we wrapped
ourselves

in each other, hearts beating as one, waiting for warmth to flow into our bodies. It had to be today;
the day the sky was bright and the air was warm. The
day the birds were singing outside my window, so I
wouldn't be cold alone.

You called me a whore and won

You called me a whore that day standing in the kitchen
with the pale yellow walls and outdated Formica countertops.
You called me a whore that day after a phone call from a man
I had been fucking when I needed a break from fights, to-do lists,
appointments and life. You called me a whore that day without
giving me a chance to explain that on that hot, humid August day
when I walked out that door with my U-Haul behind my SUV that I
was saying goodbye and leaving that life. You called me a whore
that day without knowing that I was done with the trying, exhausted
of who you thought I should be or who you wanted me to be. You called
me a whore that day because my sexual encounters with another man
didn't live up to your expectations of how a relationship should look. One

man and one woman should be together is what you said, even though
that's not how I wanted to live. So you called me a whore that day,
but then you asked me to stay and I did. Now I live with the regret
of not leaving that kitchen with the pale yellow walls and outdated
Formica countertops as the whore you said I was.

Girl on the Ledge

We walked along the tree-lined street as hues of gold and amber
fell like a soft rain gently tapping on our shoulders. You lovingly
entwined your hand in mine and laughed at my corny attempt
of a joke as we stopped at a sidewalk café, latte for me, espresso for you,
and chatted over upcoming plans to fulfill the silenced moments.

It was a day of perfection as if looking into a snow-filled globe of
happiness. In this moment there was no mind-numbing pain, only
bursts of laughter and stealing sideways glances at each other,
the way I used to sit on the ledge watching you as you took the
dog out for his morning walk, and I pretended to be reading my book.

In that moment we couldn't predict the rawness of truth that would

soon follow as our love became stale, when we would chose to let
the silence stay silent and the stealing glances change to eye-rolls
and sighs. And as you walked out our door that day, the snow-filled
globe fell and shattered on the ground and so did the girl on the ledge.

Whisky and Cigarettes

I need to learn I am more than a hollow shell, like the chocolate bunny sitting on the shelf at Easter. My body was formed with soul, not for a quick taste of pleasure that leaves a bitter taste of regret in your mouth. These hands were created for purpose, more than providing you with a moment of ecstasy. Yet, I sit here with a glass of whisky in my hand and a cigarette in my mouth asking why I allow myself to be nothing more than what you are willing to give to me. A momentary satisfaction, so brief that your smell does not even linger on my sheets. Am I ashamed of who I am? Or are you ashamed of who I am? I pick up my pillow needing to smell you one more time to prove that you were real and not someone I imagined due to loneliness. Afraid to breathe in knowing the truth that no remnants of you remain. And I tell myself, maybe that's not such a bad thing.

The day we died together

You left me to grieve for you even though you told me
not too. Shifting winds blew the leaves the wrong direction.
The weather vane spun uncontrollably, yet your slow
Death from cancer taunted me at every turn. Events conspired
to separate one from another without reprieve. Death worked
with time for the perfect moment.
Your silver tousles of wavy hair spanned like wings across
the pillow, framing your thin, pale face. The black-hooded figure
stood just out of sight, waiting. Why the fuck did you think
I wouldn't ache when left with empty arms? Shattered with grief
the moment you took your last breath. The smell of antiseptic
clinging in the air, and I knew I would not survive. Death so vile
it knocked down my broken body. A body you created, formed

within your womb, sacrificing to protect and love. We danced
to the rhythm and rhyme of each other's heartbeat. Now left
with a shell, once full of love, withered away the day you left
me for another life. Love and Death are bitter opposites we are told,
yet they are entwined together so gracefully that you know they are the same.

To My Narcissist with Love

Searching for a hand to hold, a confidant to love,
I found you to keep me in my place, you say as if it was normal

As your words of lies, spew from your mouth,
Provoking me, I still feel love, even with scars of hate I own.

I rise each day, biting at my heels to keep us forced into motion,
Upon the lonely, barren ground you claim is our ocean.

Had the ocean been my confidant, instead of you, the one I trusted,
I would have given it all my loneliness, and received a wave of emotions.

Instead I allowed you to keep me barren upon the ground I walk alone,
Drowning in the loneliness while you keep me only as a token.

A piece of waste that you found clinging to the tide in the ocean,

As I searched for a hand to hold, I found you
and a life of corrosion.

Whispers and Lullabies

I'm sorry my life didn't come with a warning
label, a symbol or a sign of caution. Danger
ahead is what my hazard would state. I'm sorry
a disaster is what my life entails. A battle won
a battle lost. Sinking ship in this storm called life
that we endure in our weakest moments. A war

you should have left behind. It was not your war
to win; I was not your soldier to save. The
warning
signs of panic were scarred on my translucent
face. Life
fed me the poison that festered in my veins.
Danger
flowed from my pores and left my withered
body unwon.
Would you have listened if I had told you I was
sorry

for the oozing disappointment that seeped out of
me? Sorry
for exposing you to sleepless, hellish nights; the
nightly wars
of smoke and fire leaving scattered ash. Hoping
for one win;

one glimpse of life remaining in the ruins of
dark. No warning
label accompanied the pile of broken bones
claimed by dangered
flesh. Bound by rumors spreading like wildfires,
disguised as life's

little whispers and lullabies, reminding me of
one more tainted life
regret. The I love you's I didn't say, or maybe I
didn't believe. Sorry,
is what I should tattoo as my label on my chest,
dangerous
arms hugging me on a cold, lonely night. Would
this protect me against these wars I fight in my
head, illusions of happiness that I crave? No one
warned
me that my mind would taunt me with the what
if's I cannot have or win.

Leave me with my shameful memories and
erratic wanderings of my unwon
mind. Leave me to spiral down, or take away the
pain and throw my life
over the edge of the bridge that draws you to me.
Don't say I didn't warn
that I would suck the last breath out of your
lungs. You will be sorry

for staying, caring, or pretending that my life
mattered to you. The war
will consume you, eat you alive and spit you out.
It will bring danger

to your soul, suck out your blood, leave you
laying on the streets in danger
alone. Don't allow my sins, my mistakes to
break you, the war to win
you. To overtake your thoughts and spin them
dragging you down. The war
will target you, chase you down until it shatters
your ability to live.
Leave before my poison exposes you, while I sit
in silence to solve this sorry
madness. This black hole of darkness
surrounding me like a cloak. No warning

as I play Russian Roulette. With bile in their
throats, people call me dangerous,
because I am a sorry dangerous girl. My body is
numb; it has fought and not won. My brain is on
fire; life has came to a close and the war has
won this round.

Puerto Vallarta

My ship ported as the sun was beginning to set for a an evening excursion that humid day in August. Vendors hollered for the cruise passengers to come look at their colorful bags and tacky t-shirts that were for sale. I quickly glanced around saying no, gracias as I passed by. I was looking for a drink, a margarita in fact, to cool myself from the smoldering heat that instantly covered my body in a glistening layer of sweat causing my sundress to cling to my thighs as I walked along the port dock.

Up ahead I saw a margarita stand, nothing more than a faded wooden counter
with a couple bar stools, and made my way to wait in line. I could already taste
the fresh lime on my lips and the tang of the salt on my tongue as I took my drink from a dark-skinned man with the softest, brown eyes and callused hands. His name was Miguel he said, as I looked him over shielding my face under my wide-brimmed hat. I didn't reply, but still he gently took my hand in his and kissed it so softly.

My body tingled from the coolness of his lips on my hand, or maybe from the unexpected touch of a man. I sat at the counter stealing glances of his movements and interactions with the other patrons. I finished my drink and stood to leave when he called out, quedar. I smiled and waved my hand no, yet he persisted, hermosa estancia de la chica. My brain screamed to go, but my body insisted I stay at that faded wooden counter on that humid day in August, waiting for a man who I would leave in three hours.

Miguel

The moon was beginning to rise as Miguel led me away from that faded wooden counter at the margarita stand. We walked along the palm-lined streets with the colorful casas, a place I knew I should not be. He took me inside his humble home and wasted no time before running those calloused hands down my body.

He spoke in Spanish, nothing I could understand, yet understanding completely. He unbuttoned my blouse and held my breasts in his hands, saying, eres una diosa, before taking them in his mouth for pleasure. I let him lead this escapade, not knowing if I had enough courage to let myself feel the freedom.

He laid me on his bed with the blue-striped blanket that smelled of sweat and cigar tobacco as his hand rested on my knee, gently sliding up my inner thigh. A chill covered my body as I looked at his face and kissed him passionately, allowing my tongue to explore his mouth, causing him to groan in ecstasy.

I allowed Miguel, a man I didn't know, to make love to me that night in his casa in Puerto Vallarta as he whispered sweet nothings in Spanish in my ear. After Miguel succeeded in his conquest, I bore my soul to him while our naked bodies lay side by side, sticky with sweat while thinking of you.

Tangled in Lesbian Lust

It started with a friendly hug, she didn't quite
know
what she was doing. A chance encounter that
quickly
turned into more, she didn't know what she was
getting herself into.
She messaged and ask to meet in person, was
she
her type? Would she be attracted to her?
Men were always more forward, ready to
pounce and
tell her how perfect her breasts were, how her
eyes
would look lovely looking up at them while
sucking
cock, how her curves would fit perfectly against
their
hard body.
But she wasn't so direct. A kiss emoji, a purple
heart,
a yes, I think you should come see me, was all
that
she would reply.
It started out with a friendly hug and a long

conversation about life before the awkwardness
set
in and the room went still. Or was that her heart
that
stopped beating out of fear? Nervousness?
Excitement? She told her to come closer,
opening her
arms. Her skin so silky, almost velvet to the
touch.
Her cheeks were warm, she could feel the heat
exchange between the two bodies.
Stealing the opportunity to kiss her lips, slipping
in
her tongue, tasting her for the first time.
Exploring Her
body with her hands, touching every inch of
skin,
memorizing every curve, the graceful contours
of her hips.
Her fingers climbed, trembling onto her
Uncharted voluptuousness breasts. She looked
into
her eyes, wrapped in the moment of unfamiliar
past
of two female lovers, learning with each kiss,
each
touch, until both were tangled in pure passion
and
lesbian lust.

Her

Be with me she whispered through the tears
Leave behind the years of regrets, fears and
failures
Love me and let me carry the darkness for you
and light me the way for the both of us.

What Remains

The sky was the color of raining fire that day.
Her eyes remained closed as she stood in the
moment
like she was frozen in time, taking in all that
filled her
mind and soul. Her body absorbed the
slow-burning
heat showering her like a warm blanket, slowly
melting the ice that her body had formed for so
many
years. Always afraid to let it chip away, away
like a
new day that was just beginning when the sun
rises in the eastern morning sky. She shivered as
the
heat hit her face and a smile emerged from
somewhere deep inside. No more cold she felt.
No
more darkness swept over here keeping the heat
at
bay. Now only strength covered her as she let go
of
the remains of him to find herself.

Falling

As a child falls into a freshly raked pile of leaves, I fell into you
Anticipation rising as the mountain of leaves build, I fell into you
Excitement overshadowing all fears and worries of the fall, I fell into you

Expecting the anticipation of the chase to keep me filled
Long after the excitement of the catch let me down
But what seems an eternity in our innocent childhood days
Escalates in warp speed in our adult years

And although the fall was not far
It broke me in the end.

Hold My Silence

You let me live in a world without knowing
that my scars are beautiful,
that my brokenness did not define me
So now you will know a world without my
presence
and hold my silence that I held for too long.

Crashing Waves

She dreams of quiet nighttime walks on the
desolate moonlit beach.
Along the black as ebony, shell-laced water,
reflecting the ivory beam.
Her tearful sorrows silenced within the sound of
the crashing billow waves.

She looks up to the wild moon child who
embraces her trembling vacant soul.
But she knows time is of the essence as morning
rises with golden rays.
She dreams of quiet nighttime walks on the
desolate moonlit beach.

As night circles back, she dreams of the moonlit
beach once more, only
the wild moon child is lost in sullen thunder
clouds cracked with bolts of light.
Her tearful sorrows silenced within the sound of
the crashing billow waves.

When it's time to wake, she wonders why her
own wild moon child has gone away.
When will her trembling vacant soul be replaced
with a womb of more than a ghost.

She dreams of quiet nighttime walks on the desolate moonlit beach.

Her sleep is fitful, her dreams are mere illusions, the sky puddles change to stars, wild moon child embraces her, "Your womb no longer remains a barren land."
Her tearful sorrows silenced within the sound of the crashing billow waves.

Finding My Religion on A Deserted, Dusty Road in A White-Washed, Wooden Country Church

With glass-stained windows, crimson, gold with hues of blue,
the old steeple gleaming in the sun, a remembrance of sin-
less love. I could hear the heavenly chorale, dressed in velvet robes,
singing the haunting, harmonious chorus of Old Gospel Hymns.
Watching over the moss-infested stones, a church full of secrets,
was the place where I first found my religion and met God.

After years of seeking silence from the beating in my chest, God,
I prayed. Not for forgiveness but rather cries of mercy blew
from my lips, for the sleazy hotel hookups and one-night stand secrets.
Attention whore, floozie, slut, is that all I was, names defining my sexual

Acts? Looking for approval and security, yet
only rank strangers to me
they left me diseased and demoralized with
fragmented promises robed

in regret. Coated with shame that burned embers
of guilt down my disrobed
body, I had forgotten long ago that life was a
privilege, not my Goddamn
personal playground. Instead using it as a way to
forget, even when it hurt,
where shots and smiles and nights of lust is all
that remained on my blueprints
of respect. My body a temple for the next Tinder
swipe, Match.com, the next Joe at the bar, flesh
covered by skin, empty underneath the scars, no
secrets

left to hide. I have no blame except to myself.
Sexting guys in secretive
moments led me to this mess alone. Alone I was,
in a wooden forest, unrobed
wearing a handprint necklace around my throat.
No more were the sins
mine alone. He left me there, exposed, as he
disposed me like he was God.
Laying there among the leaves and limbs,
staring straight-up at the blue-

less sky, still and soulless, thinking how
beautiful heaven must be.

I never even knew if you existed, if heaven was
real, but love lifted me
from that moment of doubt and the pain I had
carried was gone. Secrets
vanished and I felt serenity at last. My naked
body, cold to the touch, blue
tinted, eyes wide, covered by gashes, bruises,
blood and cuts, no robe
to cover my shame, guilt, remorse, instead I rose
in a cloak of your
love. No longer was the girl who wore the
names of whore and MeetMe

slut. No longer the abused daddy's little girl
looking for approval of men. Sin
no longer bound me in that wooden forest, naked
and ashamed. Amazing Grace
how sweet was the sound, as the choir welcomed
me home and I met you, God,
as my body lowered to the ground, where the
moss blankets the stones. Secrets
had no hold, no longer belonged, for tonight I
was born again, dressed in a robe
of gold, in a white-washed, wooden country
church, stained glass with hues of blue.

I listened as the trumpeters blew their horns,
turning my sins white as snow.
For Heaven holds no secrets and my past was all dissolved. All because you
washed my sins away, and I danced in my robe of gold near the cross.

Rubble of Darkness

Left beneath a rubble
of darkness, she claws her
way toward wind-blown skies
and wonders if he is thinking
of her too.

Baptism of Sorrow

Sorrow washed over her like a baptism in
a mountain creek on a warm summer day.
Giving her a rebirth to life, to start again when
love
was a lie that consumed her from the inside out.
Her heart ached of cold like a winter night with
freshly
fallen snow. The cold that freezes on the window
pane.
An ache to mask the pain from his deception and
deceit
Redeemed from the life that she was no longer
living.
Ready to start loving herself and wear the
sorrow proudly.

The Unstoppable Girl

She craved the outside, clawing her way to
freedom
her lungs filled with air, limbs growing strong,
body taking form to conquer the world. She was
unstoppable.
Surrounded inside her cocoon, she knew no
darkness,
faced no evil, protected by the womb. She
climbed
through the gateway marking this land as hers,
making her
voice heard, taking her stance on who she was
and who
she would become. Eager to reach what had
been denied
to her. Eager to become the woman she was
chosen to become.
She was unstoppable.
She is unstoppable.
She is a woman.

www.ingramcontent.com/pod-product-compliance
Lightning Source LLC
Chambersburg PA
CBHW051746130826
49812CB00033B/1030
9789357214780